Best Baking

First printed 2012

Eaglemoss Ltd, 1st Floor, Beaumont House,
Kensington Village, Avonmore Road,
London W14 8TS

ISSN 2049 - 6338
123456789

Printed in the EU by Cayfosa, Barcelona, Spain.

= These recipes may contain nuts or traces of nuts.

Best Baking - Grandma's puddings

Picture credits EM = Eaglemoss Ltd

06-07 Lead: EM; Steps: EM; Panel: Thinkstock
08-09 Lead: Thinkstock; Panel: Thinkstock; Step: EM
10-11 Lead: Stock Food; Panel: Thinkstock; Steps: EM
12-13 EM **14-15** EM **16-17** Stock Food **18-19** EM/Tim Hill **20-21** EM/Dairy Diary **22-23** EM/Steve Lee **24-25** EM **26-27** Stock Food **28-29** Photocuisine **30-31** EM **32-33** EM/Simon Smith **34-35** Loupe **36-37** EM **38-39** EM **40-41** EM/Dairy Diary **42-43** EM **44-45** EM **46-47** EM **48-49** EM **50-51** EM/Dairy Diary **52-53** Stock Food **54-55** Photocuisine **56-57** EM **58-59** EM/Carl Adamson **60-61** EM/Edward Allwright **62-63** Photocuisine **64-65** EM/Ken Field **66-67** Photocuisine **68-69** EM **70-71** EM **72-73** Stock Food **74-75** EM **76-77** EM **78-79** EM **80-81** EM **82-83** EM **84-85** EM/Dairy Diary **86-87** EM **88-89** EM **90-91** EM **92-93** Loupe Images **94-95** EM

Visit www.best-baking.com

UK Customer Services: Call: 0844 472 5220 **Email:** best-baking@eaglemoss-service.com
Write to: *Best Baking*, Data Base Factory, 4 Pullman Business Park, Pullman Way, Ringwood, Hampshire BH24 1HD

Australia: Call: (03) 9872 4000 **Email:** bissett@bissettmags.com.au
Write to: *Best Baking*, Bissett Magazine Service Pty Limited, PO Box 3460, Nunawading VIC 3131

New Zealand: Call: (09) 308 2871 **Email:** subs@ndc.co.nz
Write to: *Best Baking*, Netlink Subscriptions, PO Box 47-906, Ponsonby, Auckland

South Africa: Call: (011) 265 4307 **Email:** service@jacklin.co.za
Write to: Best Baking, Private Bag 18, Centurion 0046

Grandma's puddings

Made easy

Grandma's puddings

Made easy

Contents

60

68

12

44

86

56

84

48

32

Traditional puddings

Nothing beats a classic pudding just like your grandma used to make!

Baked and steamed puddings are the perfect comfort food for a chilly autumn or winter's evening. For a real classic, try our recipe opposite for a truly delicious baked jam roly-poly. Of course, the more traditional method is to steam suet puddings as it gives them a gloriously soft, open texture. But as the saying goes, grandma always knows best, which means that not only are all of her classic recipes really simple and easy to make, they lend themselves to all kinds of mouthwatering variations. So what are you waiting for? ❤

Secrets to success

Forget the cake mix, roll up your sleeves and put on an apron. With some basic know-how and simple ingredients surprise your family and friends with delicious homemade bakes.

Top tip: Custard is often the ideal choice with sponge and pastry-based puddings.

Options: Light meringues and soufflés are delicious alternatives to the stodgier puds.

Versatile: Grandma's puddings work really well at dinner parties, make them extra special and serve them as individual portions in ramekins.

Worth it: Most grandmas would always cook from scratch and not cut corners. It takes more time and effort but it's worth every second.

Baked jam roly-poly

Serves 6 **Preparation** 20 minutes + cooling **Cooking** 40 minutes

Ingredients

175g (6oz) self-raising flour
75g (3oz) shredded suet
225g (8oz) raspberry jam

1 Preheat the oven to 200°C/400°F/gas 6. Sift the flour into a bowl and stir in the suet (you can also use vegetable suet). Add enough cold water, about 150ml (¼pt), to form a soft dough.

2 Roll out a 20cm x 30cm (8in x 12in) rectangle and spread thickly with the jam, leaving a 4cm (1½in) border.

3 Brush with a little water on the pastry edges to dampen, then roll firmly from a short end.

4 Lift the roly-poly onto a greased baking tray and bake for 40 minutes or until golden.

5 Leave to stand for 10 minutes to allow the jam to cool slightly, then serve in slices with custard.

Steamed to perfection

What could be more comforting than a steamed pudding? Here's how to get it right...

Pleats: When you make the cover for your pudding from buttered greaseproof paper and foil, add a central pleat. This will allow the pudding to expand. Also tie a string handle around the pudding, to allow you to lift it out of the pan.

Equipment: If you don't have a steamer you can use a saucepan. Just turn a heatproof dish or saucer upside-down in the bottom and stand the pudding basin on it.

Danger!: Never let the water in the steamer or pan run dry. The water will evaporate quickly so check regularly and top up with more boiling water as necessary.

Crumbles and cobblers

The British crumble and the American cobbler both make simple and delicious toppings for stewed fruit puddings.

Crumbles are popular not only because they taste so good, they are also really easy to make. Another benefit is that you can be flexible with the cooking temperature. That means that if you're cooking other things in the oven at the same time – a Sunday roast perhaps – then the crumble will be fine. Apple crumble is a family favourite, but it is also worth experimenting with different fruit combinations and toppings. Or why not try the crumble's American cousin, the cobbler. This tends to have a denser scone-based topping which is then broken up into large, rough crumbs or moulded into shapes on top of a fruit base. Cobbler dough shaped into hearts, animals or stars make cute toppings for individual puddings. Crumbles and cobblers taste even better with lashings of custard, double cream or vanilla ice cream. ❤

Top toppings

Knowing how to make a standard crumble topping is vital for any home cook's baking repertoire, and there are lots of things you can do to add flavour and texture...

Basic crumble topping: The foundations of a plain crumble topping are plain flour, butter and sugar. Try out the delicious recipe on page 74.

Classic cobbler: The basic ingredients for a cobbler topping are plain flour, baking powder, sugar, butter, salt and whipping cream. See page 60 for a great recipe.

Spice it up: Both types of topping can be given extra flavour. Good things to try are spices, especially cinnamon, citrus zest and crushed nuts. Oats make a healthy addition to crumble toppings too.

Apricot and almond crumble

A delicious mix of fruit and nut make this a simply stunning crumble. Make sure you really do leave it to stand for a few minutes, though, as hot fruit can scald your mouth!

Serves 6 **Preparation** 15 minutes **Cooking** 40 minutes

Ingredients

700g (1½lb) ripe apricots
150g (5oz) caster sugar
175g (6oz) plain flour
125g (4oz) ground almonds
175g (6oz) butter, diced
50g (2oz) flaked almonds

1 Preheat the oven to 190°C/375°F/gas 5. Quarter and stone the apricots. Spread in a shallow baking dish and sprinkle with 25g (1oz) of the caster sugar.

2 For the crumble topping, mix together the remaining sugar, the flour and the ground almonds.

3 Rub in the butter until the mixture resembles breadcrumbs. Spoon the mixture evenly over the fruit and generously scatter the flaked almonds on the top.

4 Bake in the oven for 35–40 minutes. Cover the surface loosely with a sheet of foil if the almonds start to brown too quickly. Remove from the oven and leave to stand.

Fruit combinations

Apple combos: Apple works beautifully as a crumble filling and is also good mixed with other flavours. The most famous pairing has to be blackberry and apple – an autumn classic. For a more unusual fruity twosome try apple and pineapple. Another simple way to boost flavour is to add a spice like whole cloves or ground cinnamon.

Cobbler choices: Choose fruit which is tart and juicy to balance the sweet density of the crust. Try plums, cherries or blackberries. If you use sweeter fruits, such as peach or pear, add 2–3 teaspoons of lemon juice to add a slight degree of tartness.

Custard know-how

Most of grandma's puddings taste better with homemade custard...

Whether it's the kind you pour piping hot over your favourite pudding or bake into a tart, the basis for custard recipes is cream and/or milk, sugar and egg yolks. For many people, the creamy goodness of a plain vanilla custard cannot be bettered. This luscious topping goes perfectly with so many classic puddings, from crumbles to pies to steamed puddings. But once you have mastered making the traditional custard recipe, try out some of our other flavour suggestions (see page 11). There are lots of other delicious combinations too. You can experiment with adding spices, citrus fruits or alcohol. Lavender even makes a subtle and flavoursome addition to custard and goes beautifully with ginger puddings. If you're in a rush, try jazzing up shop-bought custard by stirring in some of our suggested flavours.

Secrets to success

Fear of lumps is what drives many home cooks to the supermarket in search of custard powder or ready-made custard. Follow these easy tips to avoid disaster...

Unscrambling eggs: Make sure that the base of the bowl is not in contact with the simmering water, or the custard may scramble and end up with lumps in it.

Keeping it fresh: Egg sauces readily absorb other flavours, so always keep a wooden spoon just for making desserts, or you may spoil the custard with oniony or stewy flavours!

Thickening tips: If your custard is looking thin and watery then it may require a little help from a teaspoon of cornflour, mixed smoothly into a tablespoon of water and then slowly whisked into the custard. Cook for a further few minutes until the custard thickens.

Grandma's traditional custard

This simple recipe for pouring custard will make enough to serve six hungry people.

Makes 750ml (1¼pt) **Preparation** 5 minutes **Cooking** 10–15 minutes

Ingredients

8 egg yolks

75g (3oz) caster sugar

1 vanilla pod or 1 tsp vanilla extract (optional)

300ml (½pt) full fat milk

300ml (½pt) double cream

Baker's tip
To stop a skin forming on your finished custard, place plastic wrap directly on top.

1 Place the egg yolks and sugar in a bowl and beat until they are thick and pale.

2 Split the vanilla pod in half and, using the wrong end of a teaspoon, scrape the insides into the milk and cream in a saucepan, or stir in the vanilla extract. Bring the mixture almost to the boil over a low heat.

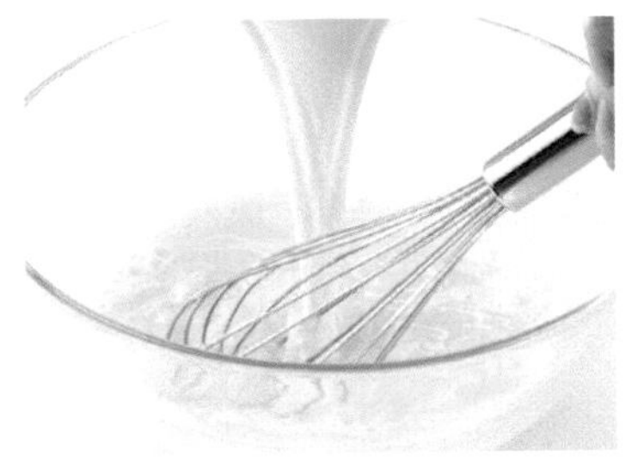

3 Whisk the milk and cream mixture into the bowl with the eggs and sugar.

4 Sit the bowl over a pan of simmering water and whisk the hot cream and milk into it. Do not overheat or boil the custard or the eggs will scramble. Keep stirring all the time until the custard leaves a thin coating on a wooden spoon – run your finger across the back of the spoon and it should leave a clear trail.

5 Sieve the custard into a jug or bowl. Serve immediately or cover and leave to cool.

Flavour ideas

Luxury chocolate: For a classic custard variation, omit the vanilla and stir 200g (7oz) of melted milk chocolate into the custard until smooth. Replace the melted chocolate with 3 tablespoons of cocoa if short on time.

Spices: Cinnamon or nutmeg add a delicious depth of flavour to plain, vanilla custard.

Banana pudding: Turn your custard into an instant dessert that'll please both children and adults by adding 1 chopped banana per person.

Sticky treacle tart

Tradition with a twist

Serves 6 **Preparation** 20 minutes + resting **Cooking** 35 minutes

Ingredients

200g (7oz) ready-made, sweet shortcrust pastry

250g (9oz) golden syrup

Zest, rind and juice of 1 orange

125g (4oz) cornflakes

Julienne strips of 1 orange zest, to decorate

1 Preheat the over to 200°C/400°F/gas 6. Roll the shortcrust pastry out and use it to line a buttered 18cm (7in) flan tin or pie dish. Rest the pastry shell in the fridge for 15 minutes.

2 Line the pastry tin with baking parchment and fill with baking beans. Bake blind for 15 minutes in the preheated oven. Remove, but leave the oven on while you make the filling.

3 Warm the golden syrup gently in a saucepan, then remove from the heat and add the orange zest and juice. Stir the mixture well to combine. Put the cornflakes in a large bowl and crush a little. Add to the syrup and orange mixture, stirring in gently.

4 Pour the filling into the pre-baked pastry shell and bake in the oven for 20 minutes until set and light golden in colour. For a finishing touch, garnish with long strips of orange rind and serve either warm or cold.

Baker's tip

Use a heavy-bottomed saucepan, watching it all the time, to gently melt the syrup.

Blackberry & apple oat crumble

Crunchy yet juicy

Serves 6 **Preparation** 20 minutes **Cooking** 1 hour

Ingredients

700g (1½lb) cooking apples, peeled and sliced
200g (7oz) blackberries
125g (4oz) granulated sugar
100g (3½oz) wholemeal flour
100g (3½oz) butter
50g (2oz) light muscovado sugar
100g (3½oz) porridge oats

1 Preheat the oven to 190°C/375°F/gas 5. Put the fruit into a 1.25 litre (2 pint) ovenproof dish in layers, sprinkling with the granulated sugar as you go.

2 Place the flour in a separate bowl and rub in the butter until the mixture resembles fine breadcrumbs. Stir in the brown sugar and porridge oats.

3 Sprinkle the crumble mixture thickly and evenly over the fruit, pressing down lightly.

4 Place the crumble dish on a baking tray and cook in the oven for 15 minutes. Reduce the temperature to 180°C/ 350°F/gas 4 and continue cooking for a further 45 minutes or until the top is lightly browned. Serve the crumble hot with custard.

Baker's tip

If you pick wild berries, pick them well away from main roads and wash them well before using.

Start your Best Baking Collection today a

nd get 4 amazing FREE gifts worth £55!

3 WAYS TO ORDER

CALL: 0844 472 5220

ORDER ONLINE: www.best-baking.com

POST: your completed coupon to us today FREE of charge

FOLD HERE

☑ **Yes!** I'd like to subscribe to the *Best Baking Collection* at £3.99 per fortnightly issue and claim my 4 fantastic FREE gifts.

- I will receive my FREE Baking Mat with my first delivery.
- I will then receive my FREE Apron with my second delivery.
- I will then receive my FREE Sifter with my third delivery.
- I will receive my FREE Cupcake Stand with my fourth delivery.
- I will receive 2 issues every 4 weeks.
- Postage and packing are free (UK only).
- I am free to cancel my subscription at any time.

Please start my subscription from issue ____

STEP 1 Details of payer

Title: Initials: Surname:

Address:

Postcode:

Telephone: ☐ Mobile: ☐

Email:

STEP 2 How to Pay

I would like to pay by:

Direct Debit ☐ Fill in the Direct Debit Form opposite Credit Card ☐ Fill in the details below

VISA ☐ MasterCard ☐ DELTA ☐ VISA Electron ☐

Card No. ☐☐☐☐ ☐☐☐☐ ☐☐☐☐ ☐☐☐☐

Start date ☐☐/☐☐ Expiry date ☐☐/☐☐

Signature ✗ Date / /

Signature of parent/guardian required if under 18

Instruction to your Bank or Building Society to pay by Direct Debit.
Please fill in the whole form and send with your completed application form to: *Best Baking Collection*, FREEPOST SWB 20869, Ringwood, BH24 1ZZ

DIRECT Debit

Name and full postal address of your Bank/Building society

To: The Manager Bank/Building Society

Address:

Postcode:

Name of Account Holder

Originator's IdentificationNumber 4 1 1 6 5 1

Branch Sort Code

Bank or Building Society Account Number

Reference Number

Please pay Eaglemoss Ltd. Direct Debits from the account detailed in this Instruction subject to the safeguards assured by the Direct Debit Guarantee. I understand that this instruction may remain with Eaglemoss Ltd and, if so, details will be passed electronically to my Bank or Building Society.

Signature ✗ Date

Banks and Building Societies may not accept Direct Debit instructions for some types of account

From time to time, *The Best Baking Collection* may publish specials issues. As a subscriber, I will automatically receive them at a discounted price. Please tick here if you do not want these. ☐

This offer is open to readers in the UK + Eire only. You may cancel this subscription request within 7 days and owe nothing. All orders subject to acceptance.

Gifts may vary and are subject to availability. Please allow 21 days for first delivery.

Eaglemoss Ltd may contact you with details of our products and services or to undertake research. Please tick here if you prefer not to receive such information by post/phone. ☐

Please tick here if you would like to receive such information by email. ☐

We occasionally pass your details onto carefully selected companies whose products and services we feel may be of interest to you. Please tick here if you prefer not to receive such information by post/ phone. Please tick here if you would like to receive such information by email. ☐

MOISTEN HERE

MOISTEN HERE

MOISTEN HERE

www.best-baking.com

NO
STAMP
NEEDED

Best Baking Collection,
FREEPOST SWB20869,
RINGWOOD,
BH24 1ZZ

Classic Bakewell tart

Sweet & nutty

Serves 6 **Preparation** 30 minutes + cooling **Cooking** 1 hour

Ingredients

- 225g (8oz) ready-made sweet shortcrust pastry
- 4 tbsp raspberry jam
- 150g (5oz) unsalted butter
- 150g (5oz) caster sugar
- 3 eggs, beaten
- 1 egg yolk
- 150g (5oz) ground almonds
- 1 tbsp flaked almonds

1 Grease a 20.5cm (8in) tart tin or flan dish. Roll out the pastry on a lightly floured surface to about 3mm (⅛in) thickness. Line the tin with the pastry, prick the base lightly with a fork and chill for 20 minutes.

2 Preheat the oven to 180°C/350°F/gas 4. Line the pastry case with baking parchment and fill with baking beans. Cook for about 20 minutes until the pastry is pale, yet golden. Remove the beans and paper and cook for a further 2 minutes. Cool slightly.

3 For the filling, spread the jam evenly over the pastry base. Beat together the butter and sugar until light and creamy. Gradually beat in the eggs and egg yolk. Stir in the ground almonds and spoon the mixture over the jam and spread level.

4 Bake for 20 minutes. Scatter with the flaked almonds and continue to cook for a further 15–20 minutes until golden. Set aside to cool. Remove from the tin and dust with icing sugar and serve with pouring cream.

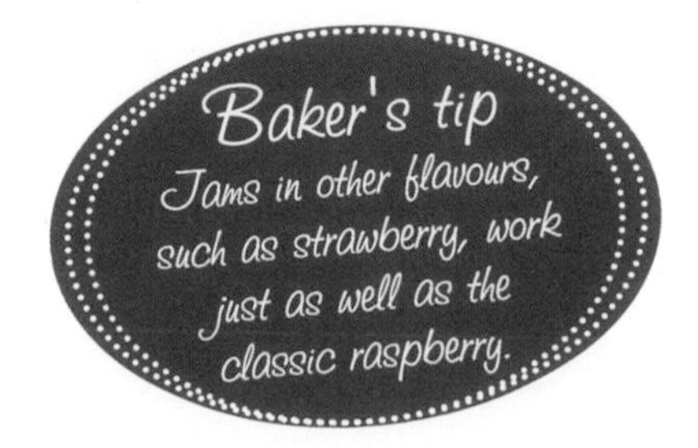

CONTAINS
NUTS

Tropical fruit pavlova

Crispy & creamy

Serves 6–8 **Preparation** 30 minutes **Cooking** 1 hour

Ingredients

3 egg whites
175g (6oz) caster sugar
1 tsp white wine or raspberry vinegar
1 tsp cornflour

For the filling

300ml (10fl oz) double cream
2 tbsp elderflower cordial
1 firm, ripe mango, diced
2 kiwi fruit, sliced
1 papaya, diced
2 passion fruit

1 Preheat the oven to 130°C/250°F/gas ½. Using a dessert plate as a guide, draw a 20.5cm (8in) circle on a sheet of baking parchment. Turn over the paper and use it to line a baking tray.

2 Put the whites into an absolutely clean, dry, large bowl and whisk the egg whites until soft peaks form. Add half the sugar and whisk until the meringue is stiff and glossy. Gradually whisk in the remaining sugar, then the vinegar and cornflour.

3 Use a metal spoon to spread the meringue within the marked circle and make a slight hollow in the centre to hold the filling later. Bake for 1 hour or until crisp outside and soft inside. Allow to cool on the baking tray. Remember to first ease the meringue case onto its serving plate before starting to fill and decorate it.

4 For the filling, whisk the cream until it is stiff, then beat in the elderflower cordial. Pile it into the hollow of the meringue case. Arrange the fruit attractively on top of the creamy filling, finish with passion fruit seeds.

Baker's tip
Take care not to break the egg yolks when separating or the yolk will prevent the white from whisking.

Chocolate sauce pudding

Intensely gooey

Serves 6 **Preparation** 10 minutes **Cooking** 50 minutes

Ingredients

175g (6oz) self-raising flour
75g (3oz) cocoa powder
75g (3oz) butter, softened
175g (6oz) golden caster sugar
200ml (7fl oz) full fat milk

For the sauce

125g (4oz) golden caster sugar
25g (1oz) cocoa powder
600ml (1pt) boiling water

1 Preheat the oven to 170°C/325°F/gas 3. Sift the flour and cocoa powder into a bowl and rub in the butter. Stir in the sugar and mix in the milk until smooth, the mixture will be quite stiff but this is how it is meant to be.

2 Spoon into a 1.75 litre (3 pint) ovenproof baking dish and level the surface. To make the sauce, mix together the sugar and cocoa and whisk in the boiling water. Pour the cocoa liquid over the pudding and bake for 40–50 minutes or until the top is firm and there is a lovely dark sauce at the bottom.

3 Leave to stand for a minute or two only before serving as the sauce will be absorbed by the fluffy sponge if left to stand for too long.

Baker's tip

The exact cooking time will depend on the depth of the dish you are using.

Bramley apple pie

Easy as pie!

Serves 8 **Preparation** 20 minutes + cooling **Cooking** 40 minutes

Ingredients

100g (3½oz) chilled unsalted butter, chopped

200g (7oz) plain flour, sifted

1 egg yolk, beaten

For the filling

18cm (7in) diameter layer of bought or home-made sponge cake, 5mm (¼in) thick

450g (1lb) Bramley apples

Juice and grated zest of 1 lemon

½ tsp grated orange zest

4 tbsp demerara sugar

½ tsp ground cinnamon

For the glaze

2 tbsp apricot jam

Baker's tip
Putting a layer of sponge in the pastry base keeps the shell crisp and firm.

1 For the pastry, rub the butter into the flour until it resembles coarse breadcrumbs. Mix in the egg to form a dough. Chill for 20 minutes. On a lightly floured surface roll out two-thirds of the pastry until it is 3mm (⅛in) thick. Use it to line an 18cm (7in) sandwich tin, leaving the excess hanging over the edge.

2 Place the sponge in the base of the pastry-lined tin, trimming it if necessary to fit. Chill until required.

3 For the filling, peel, core and chop the apples. Mix with the lemon juice and zest, orange zest, sugar and cinnamon. Spoon into the pastry case. Roll out the remaining pastry until it is 3mm (⅛in) thick. Brush the pastry edge with water, then lay the lid on top. Press down firmly with your fingers to seal.

4 Trim the pastry edge and pierce a hole in the centre top. Cut leaf shapes from the trimmings and stick to the pie with water. Preheat the oven to 200°C/400°F/gas 6 and cook for 40 minutes, then let it cool for 10 minutes.

5 Mix the jam and 4 tablespoons water in a pan. Heat until simmering, then sieve. Run a knife round the pie, then turn it out of the tin and put it on a serving plate. Brush the top with the jam glaze. Serve with hot custard.

Baked cheesecake

New York-style!

Serves 6 Preparation 20 minutes + soaking and chilling Cooking 50 minutes

Ingredients

175g (6oz) plain flour
50g (2oz) caster sugar
½ tsp grated lemon zest
75g (3oz) unsalted butter, diced
1 large egg yolk
1 tbsp brandy

For the filling

50g (2oz) sultanas
2 tbsp dark rum
450g (1lb) white curd cheese (or full-fat cream cheese)
142ml carton double cream
½ lemon, juice only
3 eggs, beaten
50g (2oz) caster sugar
Icing sugar, to dust

Baker's tip
As the pastry is crumbly, it might break. If it does, just press firmly into the tin and trim any excess.

1 For the filling, put the sultanas into a bowl and pour over the rum. Leave to soak for 2 hours.

2 For the pastry, mix the flour, sugar, lemon zest. Add the butter and rub in with fingertips until the mixture resembles fine breadcrumbs. Make a well in the centre and add the egg yolk and brandy. Bring together to form a dough. Turn out onto a floured surface and knead gently until smooth. Wrap in plastic wrap and chill for at least 30 minutes.

3 Preheat the oven to 200°C/400°F/gas 6. To complete the filling, put the curd cheese in a bowl, then add cream and lemon juice. Stir in the eggs and sugar.

4 Line a 20cm (8in) deep flan tin with the pastry. Sprinkle with the sultanas and rum. Pour the cheesecake mixture over.

5 Put onto a baking tray and bake for 10 minutes, then reduce oven temperature to 180°C/350°F/gas 4 and bake for a further 35–40 minutes until the mixture is set in the centre and the cheesecake is golden brown. Leave the cheesecake to cool slightly, remove from tin and cool on a wire rack. Dust lightly with icing sugar and serve.

Strawberry roulade

A creamy classic

Serves 8 **Preparation** 30 minutes + cooling **Cooking** 12 minutes

Ingredients

3 eggs
75g (3oz) caster sugar, plus extra for sprinkling
75g (3oz) plain flour, sifted twice
Icing sugar, to decorate
Sprigs of mint, to decorate

For the filling

300ml (½pt) double cream
50g (2oz) icing sugar
200g (7oz) strawberries, sliced
2 tbsp strawberry liqueur (optional)

Baker's tip
When rolling up, don't worry too much if a few cracks appear, it's all part of the charm!

1 Preheat the oven to 220°C/425°F/gas 7. For the sponge, grease a 20cm x 30cm (8in x 12in) Swiss roll tin and line with non-stick baking parchment. Put the eggs and sugar in a heatproof bowl. Set over a pan of simmering, but not boiling, water and whisk until the mixture is thick, creamy and leaves a trail. Gently fold in the flour.

2 Pour the mixture into the tin and bake for 10–12 minutes, until risen and golden. Remove from the oven and turn out onto non-stick baking parchment sprinkled with sugar. Trim the sponge edges and roll up with the paper inside. Leave to cool completely.

3 For the filling, whisk the cream and icing sugar until thick. Stir in the strawberries and liqueur, if using. Unroll the sponge, remove the paper and spread the filling evenly over the sponge. Roll up carefully and place on a serving plate. Sift the icing sugar over the top.

Lemon meringue

Citrus classic

Serves 6 Preparation 1 hour + cooling Cooking 40 minutes

Ingredients

225g (8oz) ready-made shortcrust pastry

2 tbsp cornflour

100g (3½oz) caster sugar

Finely grated zest of 2 lemons

125ml (4fl oz) lemon juice

Juice of 1 small orange

75g (3oz) butter, cubed

3 egg yolks, plus 1 whole egg

For the meringue

4 egg whites, at room temperature

200g (7oz) caster sugar

2 tsp cornflour

1 Preheat the oven to 200°C/400°F/gas 6. Roll the pastry out on a lightly floured surface and line a 23cm x 2.5cm (9in x 1in) shallow pie dish. Prick the base with a fork and line with baking parchment. Fill with baking beans and blind bake for 12–15 minutes. Remove the parchment and beans and bake for a further 5–7 minutes until pale golden. Turn the oven down to 180°C/350°F/gas 4. Set to one side and allow to cool.

2 For the filling, mix the cornflour, sugar and lemon zest in a pan. Add the lemon juice and make the orange juice up to 200ml (7fl oz) by adding water. Heat over a medium flame, stirring constantly until it thickens. Once it starts to bubble, remove from the heat and beat in the butter. Beat the egg yolks and whole egg into the mixture. Return to a gentle heat and cook, stirring until thickened. Remove from the heat and cool slightly then pour into the pastry case.

3 For the meringue, whisk the egg whites in a large clean bowl to soft peaks and then whisk in half the sugar, a tablespoon at a time. Whisk in the cornflour, then the remaining sugar by the tablespoon. Spoon the meringue onto the lemon filling and swirl. Bake for 20 minutes until the meringue is golden. Leave to cool for 1 hour and serve.

Crème caramel

Silky smooth

Serves 6 **Preparation** 40 minutes + cooling **Cooking** 1 hour 15 minutes

Ingredients

75g (3oz) granulated sugar
3 tbsp water

For the custard

3 eggs, plus 3 egg yolks
50g (2oz) sugar
½ tsp vanilla essence
600ml (1pt) milk

1 Preheat the oven to 160°C/325°F/gas 3. To make the caramel, put sugar and water in a heavy-based pan and heat gently, stirring until the sugar dissolves. Raise heat and boil for 5–10 minutes, without stirring, until amber-coloured.

2 Warm a 1 litre (1¾ pint) soufflé dish in the oven. When the caramel is ready, dunk the base of the saucepan in cold water to stop it cooking. Pour caramel into the soufflé dish, turning to coat sides, leaving a thick layer in the base.

3 To make the custard, whisk the eggs, yolks and sugar with the vanilla essence. Heat the milk until it begins to boil, then cool it a little and pour it into the egg mixture, stirring continously.

4 Place the caramel-lined soufflé dish into a deep roasting tin. Strain the custard into the dish. Pour hot water into the tin, to come halfway up the soufflé dish. Bake for about 1 hour.

5 When set, leave the crème caramel to cool. Run the tip of a knife round the inside of the dish to loosen the custard – especially to free the top edge if it is stuck to the dish. Place a serving dish with a high lip or rim over the soufflé dish. Invert quickly, then lift the soufflé dish carefully off the crème caramel and serve immediately.

Baker's tip

For the right texture, remove the custard from the oven while it is still wobbly in the centre.

Baked Alaska

Sensational dessert!

Serves 6–8 **Preparation** 1 hour + chilling **Cooking** 25 minutes

Ingredients

175g (6oz) fresh raspberries
700g (1½lb) good quality vanilla ice cream, softened

For the chocolate sponge

75g (3oz) butter, softened
75g (3oz) caster sugar
1 egg
50g (2oz) self-raising flour
25g (1oz) cocoa powder
½ tsp baking powder

For the meringue

3 egg whites
150g (5oz) caster sugar
25g (1oz) icing sugar for dusting

Baker's tip
Ensure your oven is at the correct high temperature, if not the meringue will not brown quickly enough.

1 Line a 1 litre (1¾ pint) pudding basin with two layers of plastic wrap. Press well into the basin, removing any air bubbles. Crush half the raspberries with a fork. Beat them into the softened ice cream then fold in the whole ones. Work quickly to avoid the ice cream melting. Put the mixture into the basin, cover with a piece of plastic wrap and put into the freezer – it needs to be frozen solid.

2 Preheat the oven to 180°C/350°F/gas 4. Put all the sponge ingredients into a large bowl or a food processor and whisk until the mixture is smooth and creamy. Scrape it into an 18cm (7in) sponge tin, smooth the top and bake for 15–18 minutes. Cool for a few minutes in the tin, then turn onto a wire rack until it is cold.

3 When the ice cream is fully set, make the meringue. Preheat the oven to 220°C/425°F/gas 7. Whisk the egg whites until they form soft peaks, then gradually beat in the sugar and whisk until the mixture forms stiff peaks. Place the circle of chocolate sponge on a non-stick baking tray. Invert the ice cream dome onto the circle. Peel off the plastic wrap and trim the sponge to fit the ice cream dome. Quickly cover with the meringue, swirling shapes into it with a palette knife.

4 When covered, bake for 6–8 minutes until the meringue is golden. Dust with icing sugar and serve immediately.

Steamed sticky toffee pudding

A modern classic

Makes 6 **Preparation** 20 minutes **Cooking** 1 hour 30 minutes

Ingredients

100ml (3½fl oz) dulce de leche
125g (4oz) butter
125g (4oz) caster sugar
2 eggs
125g (4oz) self-raising flour
1 tbsp instant coffee dissolved in 1 tbsp boiling water
40g (1½oz) walnut pieces
Double cream or vanilla ice cream, to serve

1 Pour the dulce de leche into greased 150ml (¼ pint) pudding bowls. Beat together the butter and sugar until pale and creamy, then beat in the eggs, one at a time. Sift over the flour and fold in, then stir in the coffee followed by the walnuts. Pour the mixture into the individual moulds.

2 Cover each mould with 2 sheets of aluminium foil and tie firmly in place with a piece of string. Put the moulds in a large pan and pour boiling water into the pan about two-thirds of the way up the sides of the moulds. Cover with a lid and simmer gently for about 1 hour 30 minutes, checking the water level occasionally and topping up if necessary.

3 To serve, remove the foil, invert the moulds onto serving plates and lift off. Serve with plenty of double cream or ice cream.

Baker's tip

Dulce de leche, a soft, toffee sauce from South America, can be found in most large supermarkets.

CONTAINS NUTS

Brioche bread pudding

Classic with a twist

Serves 6–8 **Preparation** 20 minutes + soaking **Cooking** 1 hour 20 minutes

Ingredients

- 450g (1lb) brioche
- 600ml (1pt) milk
- Juice and grated zest of 1 orange
- 350g (12oz) prunes, cut in half
- 3 tbsp brandy
- 125g (4oz) butter, melted, plus extra for greasing
- 175g (6oz) light brown sugar plus extra for the topping
- 2 eggs
- ½ tsp cinnamon
- Julienne strips of 1 orange zest, to decorate

Baker's tip

Butter the loaf tin well as the mixture develops a crust which can easily get stuck to the tin.

1 Cut the crusts off the brioche and tear the rest into small chunks. Put them in a bowl, pour on the milk and leave to stand for 30 minutes. Heat the orange juice gently in a pan until hot then pour over the prunes in a separate bowl. Add the brandy and cover the bowl, then set aside to soak.

2 Preheat the oven to 180°C/350°F/gas 4. After the brioche and milk have been soaking for 30 minutes, beat the mixture until it is smooth. Then stir in the melted butter.

3 Stir in the sugar and eggs and mix well until thoroughly blended. It will look rather like a pale brown porridge at this stage. Then tip the prunes, orange juice and zest into the mixture and stir well again to distribute the prunes as evenly as possible.

4 Pour the mixture into a greased 900g (2lb) loaf tin, lined with baking parchment. Sprinkle the cinnamon and 1 tablespoon light brown sugar over the top of the pudding. Bake for about 1 hour 15 minutes until it is well risen and golden and a skewer comes out clean. Leave to cool in the tin for 10 minutes, then transfer to a wire rack. It is best served warm with strips of orange zest and a generous dollop of cream.

Boozy baked apples

Classic pudding

Serves 4 **Preparation** 15 minutes + chilling **Cooking** 30 minutes

Ingredients

15g (½oz) butter

1 tbsp granulated sugar

4 Cox's apples

2 tbsp Calvados (apple liqueur)

For the filling

125g (4oz) marzipan, finely diced

75g (3oz) white grapes, quartered

25g (1oz) chopped walnuts, toasted

1 tbsp granulated sugar

1 Preheat the oven to 180°C/350°F/gas 4. Butter an ovenproof dish, sprinkle sugar over the base. Core the apples and set aside. For the filling, mix together the marzipan, grapes, walnuts and sugar. Using a teaspoon, fill each cored apple with the mixture and arrange in dish.

2 Bake apples for 15 minutes. Take out of the oven and spoon over Calvados. Bake for a further 15 minutes, until tender. Remove from oven and set aside.

3 Place a baked apple on each plate and serve warm with a generous dollop of whipped cream.

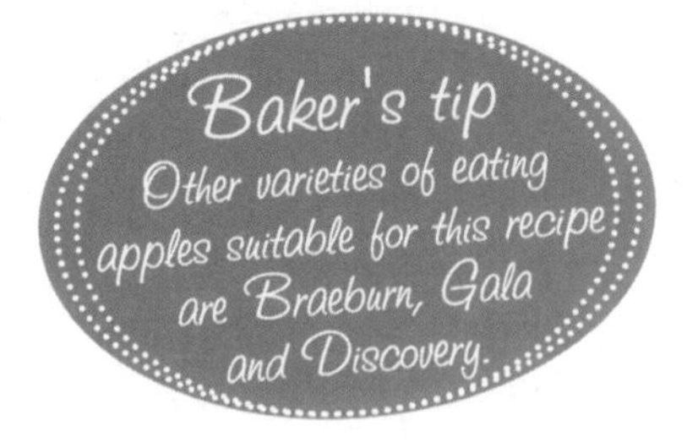

!
CONTAINS
NUTS

Banana surprise puddings

Steamed to perfection

Serves 6 Preparation 30 minutes Cooking 40 minutes

Ingredients

2 small bananas
2 tbsp sultanas
1 tbsp golden syrup

For the sponge

125g (4oz) unsalted butter
150g (5oz) caster sugar
1 vanilla pod, split and pulp scraped out
Finely grated zest and juice of ½ a lemon
2 eggs, plus 1 extra yolk
200g (7oz) self-raising flour
1 peeled orange, chopped

For the topping

2 tbsp golden syrup, plus extra for drizzling
2 oranges, peeled and cut into segments

1 Cut the bananas in 5mm (¼in) slices and gently mix with the sultanas and syrup to make the banana mixture.

2 To make the sponge, beat the butter with the sugar, vanilla pulp and lemon zest until the mixture is almost white. Beat in the eggs and egg yolk. Gently fold in the flour, lemon juice and orange pieces.

3 Spoon the 1 teaspoon of golden syrup into the greased bases of six 300ml (½ pint) pudding moulds. Fill the bottom third of each mould with the sponge mixture, then some banana mixture, and top to three-quarters full with sponge.

4 Cover the moulds with buttered foil and place in a pan half-full of boiling water or in the top of a steamer. Cover with a tight fitting lid. Steam the puddings for about 40 minutes. Top with extra golden syrup and serve with the orange segments.

Chocolate roulade

Pure indulgence!

Serves 6–8 **Preparation** 20 minutes + cooling **Cooking** 25 minutes

Ingredients

5 large eggs, separated

175g (6oz) caster sugar

175g (6oz) plain chocolate, melted, plus 1 small bar to decorate

For the filling

300ml (½pt) double cream

2 tbsp icing sugar, plus extra for dusting

4–6 tbsp Irish cream liqueur

Baker's tip

If the chocolate does not curl easily, warm in a microwave in 20-second bursts until curls form easily.

1 Preheat the oven to 180°C/350°F/gas 4. Grease and line a Swiss roll tin with baking parchment. Whisk the egg whites until stiff. Place the egg yolks and caster sugar together in a separate bowl, then whisk together until the mixture leaves a trail. Fold the melted chocolate into the egg yolk mixture then fold in the egg whites.

2 Pour the mixture into a Swiss roll tin, lined with baking parchment. Use a palette knife to lightly spread the mixture out to the edges. Bake the roulade in the centre of the oven for 20–25 minutes, or until the mixture has just set in the centre. Remove from the oven, leave it in the tin and cover with a clean, damp tea towel. Leave to cool for at least 4 hours.

3 To make the filling, whip the cream until it forms soft peaks, then fold in the icing sugar and Irish cream liqueur to taste. Dust a sheet of baking parchment with icing sugar and turn the roulade out onto it. Peel away the lining paper from the roulade and spread over the cream. Roll up using the paper to help.

4 Keep the roulade chilled until ready to serve. Use a swivel-bladed vegetable peeler to make the chocolate curls. Before serving, dust with a little extra icing sugar and scatter over the curls.

Rice pudding

An absolute classic

Serves 6 **Preparation** 30 mins + cooling **Cooking** 2 hours 5 minutes

Ingredients

1 vanilla pod
900ml (1½pt) milk
100g (3½oz) pudding rice
3 tbsp double cream
Knob of butter
15g (½oz) caster sugar
2 egg yolks
Mint leaves, to decorate

For the sauce

225g (8oz) raspberries
50ml (2fl oz) water
50g (2oz) caster sugar
Juice of 1 orange
Icing sugar, for taste

Baker's tip
Why not add more flavour to the cooked rice? Try adding orange zest before baking.

1 Split the vanilla pod and scrape the seeds into the milk in a pan. Add the rice and bring slowly to the boil. Simmer for 30–35 minutes. Remove from the heat and allow to cool. Preheat the oven to 180°C/350°F/gas 4.

2 Add the cream, butter, sugar and egg yolks to the rice and mix thoroughly. Pour the mixture into a shallow 1.2–1.7 litre (2–3 pint) lightly buttered ovenproof dish and bake for 1 hour 30 minutes until most of the liquid has been absorbed and a golden-brown skin forms.

3 While the pudding is baking, make the fruit sauce. Simmer the raspberries, water and sugar until the fruit is very tender. Allow the mixture to cool slightly then pass it through a sieve to remove any pips. Return to the pan and boil to reduce in volume by about half.

4 Cool the sauce a little and stir in the orange juice. Taste for sweetness and add icing sugar if it seems too tart. Cool the sauce completely before serving.

5 Use a ring mould or cookie cutter to cut circular portions from the pudding. Serve warm with the cold raspberry and orange sauce drizzled around and a few sprigs of mint to decorate.

Traditional sherry trifle

Old-fashioned favourite

Serves 6 **Preparation** 1 hour + cooling **Cooking** 35 minutes

Ingredients

3 eggs

100g (3½oz) caster sugar

75g (3oz) plain flour

40g (1½oz) unsalted butter, melted

Raspberry jam

For the syrup

125g (4oz) caster sugar

150ml (¼pt) water

4–5 tbsp sweet sherry

For the custard

40g (1½oz) custard powder

40g (1½oz) caster sugar

600ml (1pt) milk

For the filling and topping

300ml (½pt) double or whipping cream, whipped

125g (4oz) plain chocolate, grated into shavings

1 Preheat the oven to 200°C/400°F/gas 6. To make the sponge, whisk the eggs and sugar in a bowl over a pan of hot water until doubled in bulk and creamy. Fold in the flour and melted butter. Pour the mix carefully into a 20.5cm (8in) sponge tin and bake in the preheated oven for 25 minutes. Turn out on to a wire rack and leave to cool.

2 To make the syrup, boil the sugar and water together for about 2 minutes, then add sherry to taste. Make the custard, using custard powder, sugar and milk and following the instructions on the packet. Or make your own custard (see instructions on page 11).

3 Split the sponge in half horizontally and spread jam on both pieces. Place one half into a large glass serving bowl and soak with half of the sherry syrup. Sit the other sponge on top, jam side up, and soak with the remaining sherry syrup.

4 Pour the custard evenly over the sponge. Cover with buttered greaseproof paper to stop a skin forming and set aside for at least half an hour to cool. Then put in the fridge to set the custard. When the custard has set completely, spread the whipped cream on top. Put back into the fridge to chill. Just before serving, sprinkle the chocolate shavings generously over the cream.

Almond pear puffs

Worth the effort!

Serves 6 **Preparation** 35 minutes + cooling **Cooking** 40 minutes

Ingredients

6 pears, peeled, stalks left on
Juice of ½ lemon
1 vanilla pod
350g (12oz) caster sugar
450ml (16fl oz) water
550g (1¼lb) ready-made puff pastry
2 egg yolks

For the frangipane filling

125g (4oz) unsalted butter
125g (4oz) caster sugar
2 eggs
75g (3oz) ground almonds
Zest and juice of 2 lemons
25g (1oz) plain flour

Baker's tip
These puffs are delicious served with cream, ice cream or a drizzle of warmed golden syrup.

1 Sit the pears in a saucepan, sprinkle with lemon juice, then add the vanilla pod, sugar and water. Bring to the boil and simmer for 8 minutes. Leave the pears to cool.

2 For the frangipane, cream together the butter and sugar. Beat in one egg at a time, adding some ground almonds with each egg to help it combine. Add the grated lemon zest, then fold in the remaining ground almonds and flour. In a separate pan, boil the lemon juice until it is reduced by half and mix with the frangipane until smooth.

3 Remove the cool pears from the syrup and core from the base with an apple corer. Leave the pears to drain on a cloth. Preheat the oven to 200°C/400°F/gas 6.

4 Roll the pastry into a 60cm x 18cm (24in x 7in) rectangle and brush with egg yolk. Trim the pastry with a knife to get a straight edge. Cut into 6 long strips each 3cm (1¼in) wide. Fill the pears with frangipane. Wind a pastry strip, egg-glazed side out, round each pear from base to stalk, overlapping the coils. Trim off any excess and pinch the pastry around the stalks at the top.

5 Stand pears on a greased baking tray and refrigerate for 20–30 minutes. Bake in the preheated oven for 20–30 minutes until golden brown and well puffed up.

!
CONTAINS
NUTS

Pineapple upside-down pudding

Juicy and fruity

Serves 6 **Preparation** 15 minutes **Cooking** 35 minutes

Ingredients

- 4 tbsp golden syrup
- 227g can of 4 pineapple rings, drained
- 5 glacé cherries, halved
- 100g (3½oz) butter, softened
- 100g (3½oz) caster sugar
- 2 eggs
- 100g (3½oz) self-raising flour, sifted

1 Preheat the oven to 180°C/350°F/gas 4. Grease and line with baking parchment a 20.5cm (8in) sandwich tin. Spoon in the golden syrup and arrange the pineapple rings and nine glacé cherry halves in the base. One in each ring, one in the centre and four around the edge, one between each ring. Place the glacé cherries cut side up so that when the finished pudding is turned out, it is the outside of the cherry that you see.

2 Cream together the butter and sugar until light and fluffy, add the eggs one at a time with a little of the flour, then fold in the rest of the flour.

3 Spread the mixture evenly over the pineapple. Bake for about 35 minutes until just firm and golden. Leave the pudding in the tin for a few minutes then turn out and serve hot or cold with custard or cream.

Baker's tip

Soften the golden syrup by standing the open tin in a pan of hot water for a few minutes.

Spotted dick with maple syrup

Classic with a twist

Makes 4 **Preparation** 20 minutes **Cooking** 1 hour 30 minutes

Ingredients

3 tbsp maple syrup, plus extra for drizzling
350g (12oz) self-raising flour
125g (4oz) shredded suet
125g (4oz) caster sugar
Pinch of salt
125g (4oz) currants
Finely grated zest of 1 orange,
150ml (¼pt) milk
Candied orange peel, cut into thin strips, to decorate

1 Grease 4 individual 175ml (6fl oz) pudding basins and spoon in the maple syrup. Mix together the flour, suet, sugar, salt, currants and orange zest in a mixing bowl and stir well. Pour in the milk and mix to a soft dropping consistency.

2 Spoon the mixture into the basins, leaving room for the puddings to rise and smooth the tops. Cover with greaseproof paper with a single pleat down the centre to allow for expansion, then with a layer of pleated foil. Tie securely with string and place in a large pan and pour in boiling water to come halfway up the basins.

3 Cover and cook for 1 hour 30 minutes, topping up with boiling water as needed, until risen and spongy to the touch. Turn out and decorate with candied orange peel. Serve with maple syrup.

Baker's tip
Vegetarians can use vegetable suet, which is available in most supermarkets.

Chocolate soufflé

Light & fluffy

Makes 4 **Preparation** 20 minutes + cooling **Cooking** 30 minutes

Ingredients

- 25g (1oz) unsalted butter, for greasing
- 125g (4oz) golden caster sugar, plus extra for coating
- 2 tbsp cocoa powder, sifted, plus extra for coating
- 125ml (4fl oz) double cream
- 1 tbsp cornflour, sifted
- 1 tbsp plain flour, sifted
- 125ml (4fl oz) full-fat milk
- 2 medium egg yolks
- 4 medium egg whites
- Pinch of salt
- 1 tbsp icing sugar, to garnish

Baker's tip
Before baking, run your thumb around the insides of the ramekin rims to help the soufflés rise.

1 Brush 4 ceramic ramekins with the butter. Add a teaspoon of sugar and cocoa powder to each, coating the insides. Tip out any excess and chill until needed.

2 Whisk together the cream, cornflour, cocoa and flour in a bowl until smooth. Heat the milk in a pan over a medium heat until it comes to the boil. Remove from the heat, whisk continuously into the cream mixture. Transfer back to the pan and heat over a gentle heat, whisking until it thickens. Remove from the heat and set to one side.

3 Whisk the egg yolks and sugar until pale. Whisk the hot milk and cream into the egg yolks and sugar until smooth and transfer back to the saucepan. Cook over a gentle heat, stirring all the time, until thick. Remove from the heat, spoon into a clean bowl, leave to cool.

4 In a separate, clean mixing bowl, beat the egg whites with a pinch of salt into soft peaks. Preheat the oven to 180°C/350°F/gas 4. Once the custard mixture has cooled, stir in one-quarter of the egg whites before gently folding in the rest of the egg whites, working quickly. Spoon into the chilled ramekins and level off using a palette knife. Place on a baking tray and bake for 10–15 minutes until the soufflés are risen. Remove from the oven and dust with icing sugar. Serve immediately.

Apricot Charlotte

Fruity pockets

Makes 4 Preparation 25 minutes + cooling Cooking 25 minutes

Ingredients

- 125g (4oz) butter, softened
- 900g (2lb) fresh apricots, halved and stoned, cut into 1cm (½in) pieces
- 50g (2oz) caster sugar
- 2 tbsp apricot jam
- 450g (1lb) brioche
- Sprigs of mint, to decorate

1 Preheat the oven to 220°C/425°F/gas 7. Melt a knob of the butter in a saucepan and add the apricots. Stir them over a low heat for 1–2 minutes, then stir in the sugar.

2 After another minute, take the pan off the heat, the apricots should still be firm, and stir in the apricot jam. Taste for sweetness and add more jam if necessary, then leave to cool.

3 While the fruit is cooling, cut the brioche into 1cm (½in) slices. Using a 6cm (2½in) biscuit cutter, stamp out 4 small discs for lining the mould bases and using a 7.5cm (3in) biscuit cutter, cut 4 larger ones for covering the tops.

4 Trim the crusts off the remaining slices of brioche and cut them into fingers 3cm (1¼in) wide. Butter these fingers and the discs of brioche on one side only. Place the smaller discs, butter side down, in the base of 4 x 8cm (3¼in) metal mini-pudding moulds and line the sides with overlapping soldiers, again arranged buttered side out.

5 Divide the apricots between the 4 moulds, then top with the larger discs, buttered side up. Fold any stray brioche over the discs to seal the lid. Bake for 15–20 minutes until golden and crispy. Decorate with the sprigs of mint and serve with cream if you wish.

Baker's tip

To turn out, place a plate upside down over a mould and turn over together. Shake firmly to release.

Strawberry shortcake

Delicious treat

Serves 6 **Preparation** 20 minutes + chilling **Cooking** 30 minutes

Ingredients

125g (4oz) unsalted butter, softened

75g (3oz) caster sugar

2 egg yolks

175g (6oz) plain flour

75g (3oz) ground rice or rice flour

For the filling

300ml (½pt) double cream

1 vanilla pod

50g (2oz) icing sugar, sifted plus extra for dredging

225g (8oz) strawberries

Sprig of mint to decorate

Baker's tip

Adding egg yolks to the mix turns shortbread into the softer shortcake.

1 Cream the butter and sugar together until they are fluffy, then beat in the egg yolks. Sift in the plain flour and the ground rice or rice flour and fold it into the mixture very gently until it forms a ball of dough. Do not overwork at this stage or the shortcake will become heavy.

2 Draw a 20.5cm (8in) circle onto greaseproof paper and cut it out to use as a template for the cake. Divide the dough in half and on a floured surface roll out one piece to fit onto the paper circle. Cut round the edges with a sharp knife to neaten. Repeat with the other half of the dough. Put the shortcakes onto a greased baking sheet and chill in the fridge for 30 minutes.

3 Preheat the oven to 160°C/325°F/gas 3. Bake the shortcakes for 30 minutes or until pale golden brown. Allow them to cool for a few minutes before carefully transferring them from the baking sheet to a wire rack.

4 Put the cream into a bowl, split the vanilla pod and use a knife to scrape its seeds into the cream. Add the icing sugar and whip the cream into soft peaks. Spread one of the shortbread circles with whipped cream and strawberries and sandwich the other one on top. Dredge thickly with icing sugar and decorate with a sprig of mint.

Redcurrant & pear cobbler

Family favourite

Serves 8 **Preparation** 35 minutes **Cooking** 35 minutes

Ingredients

350g (12oz) redcurrants, pulled off their stalks

½ tsp ground cinnamon

Pinch of ground cloves

150g (5oz) caster sugar

1 tsp cornflour

5 medium pears

For the topping

150g (5oz) wholemeal plain flour

75g (3oz) plain flour

1 tsp baking powder

150g (5oz) caster sugar, plus extra for dredging

125g (4oz) unsalted butter, cut into small pieces, plus extra for greasing

100ml (3½fl oz) whipping cream

1 Preheat the oven to 200°C/400°F/gas 6. Place the redcurrants, cinnamon and cloves in a pan and add 125ml (4fl oz) water. Heat the mixture for 1–2 minutes until it boils and the currants burst, stirring occasionally. Add the caster sugar to the mixture and simmer for a further minute or two, stirring until the sugar has dissolved. Mix the cornflour with a little water until smooth. Off the heat, stir into the fruit mixture, return to a low heat and cook until the juices thicken, stirring constantly.

2 Peel the pears, cut each in half lengthways, remove the cores and slice fairly thinly. In a large greased ovenproof baking dish, arrange the pear slices into a thick layer. Spoon the redcurrant mixture over the pears, covering in an even layer but do not mix the two fruits too much.

3 For the topping, mix the flours, baking powder and caster sugar. Add the butter and cut in with a round-bladed knife until it resembles fine breadcrumbs. Add the whipping cream and stir gently with a fork until the dough leaves the sides of the bowl. Do not over-mix the dough; it should be lumpy and uneven.

4 Crumble the mixture over the fruit in an even layer. Dredge the top with caster sugar. Bake for 25-30 minutes until the topping is golden. Serve immediately.

Baked apple custards

Pudding perfection

Serves 4 Preparation 15 minutes Cooking 25–30 minutes

Ingredients

8 medium egg yolks

75g (3oz) caster sugar

1 tbsp cornflour

500ml (18fl oz) whipping cream

4 eating apples, cored and finely sliced

1 Preheat the oven to 150°C/300°F/gas 2. Whisk together the egg yolks, sugar and cornflour until pale and thick.

2 Add the cream and mix well, then pass through a fine sieve into a saucepan and heat over a medium heat, stirring all the time.

3 Arrange the apple slices in a fanned out circle in individual ovenproof dishes. Carefully pour over the custard, then transfer to the oven and bake for 20–25 minutes until the custard is set and the edges are starting to colour. Serve immediately.

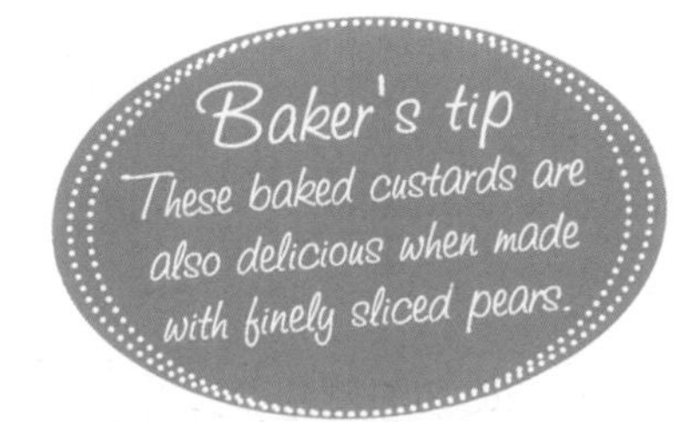

Boozy bread & butter pudding

Golden oldie!

Serves 6–8 **Preparation** 30 minutes + soaking **Cooking** 30 minutes

Ingredients

- 50g (2oz) ready-to-eat dried apricots, finely chopped
- 50g (2oz) chopped candied orange peel
- 100ml (3½fl oz) Grand Marnier®
- 50g (2oz) unsalted butter, softened, plus extra for greasing
- 12 medium-cut slices white bread
- 8 egg yolks
- 175g (6oz) caster sugar
- ½ tsp vanilla essence
- 300ml (½pt) milk
- 300ml (½pt) double cream
- Caster sugar, to glaze

Baker's tip
Test if the pudding is ready by pressing its top with your fingers, it should be firm yet springy.

1 Put the chopped apricots and candied orange peel in a bowl and pour over the Grand Marnier®. Cover the bowl with plastic wrap and leave to marinate overnight.

2 Butter the slices of bread, cut off the crusts and then cut each slice into four triangles. Drain the soaked fruit, reserving the liqueur. Lay one-third of the bread triangles in a well-buttered 1.75 litre (3 pint) baking dish, buttered side up, overlapping the triangles. Scatter over half the soaked fruit and cover with another layer of bread. Finish with the remaining fruit and a final layer of bread.

3 Whisk together the egg yolks, sugar and vanilla until the mixture is pale and it leaves a visible trail. Heat the milk, cream and reserved liqueur in a saucepan until it is just coming to the boil. Pour into the egg yolk mixture, whisking all the time. Pour over the bread so all the triangles are coated, then set aside to soak for 30 minutes.

4 Preheat the oven to 180°C/350°F/gas 4. Sit the dish in a roasting tin and pour hot water around the dish until the tin is about three-quarters full. Bake for 25 minutes or until it begins to set. Lift the dish out of the roasting tin and sprinkle the top of the pudding with a generous layer of caster sugar. Pop the dish under a hot grill for 2–3 minutes until the surface caramelises to a rich brown.

Apple tarte tatin

Continental classic

Serves 6 **Preparation** 15 minutes **Cooking** 50 minutes

Ingredients

125g (4oz) butter

125g (4oz) caster sugar

8 Golden Delicious apples, peeled cored and halved

150g (5oz) ready-made puff pastry

A little plain flour

1 Preheat the oven to 200°C/400°F/gas 6. Heat the butter and sugar over a medium-high heat in a 20.5cm (8in) ovenproof frying pan. Swirl the pan to combine the butter and sugar and continue cooking until you reach a toffee-coloured caramel.

2 Turn the heat down and add the apple halves to the pan, tucking them tightly in around the perimeter and then filling the centre. Continue cooking on a lower heat for 8–10 minutes, while you roll the pastry out on a lightly floured surface to 1cm (½in) thickness. Prick a few times with a fork.

3 Cut a round of pastry that is slightly larger than the diameter of the pan you are using. Remove the pan from the heat and carefully drape the pastry over the pan, tucking the overhanging pastry in around the edges to secure it. Transfer the pan to the oven and bake for 20–25 minutes until the pastry is risen and golden brown in colour.

4 Remove from the oven and let the tart sit for 10 minutes before running a sharp knife around the edge to loosen it a little. Place a large plate on top of the pastry and invert quickly and carefully to release the tart onto the plate. Serve immediately with cream or ice cream.

Baker's tip

When turning the tarte to serve, the frying pan will be extremely hot so always use oven gloves!

Mini chocolate custards

Creamy & rich

Makes 8 **Preparation** 40 minutes + cooling **Cooking** 40 minutes

Ingredients

125g (4oz) good quality dark chocolate, chopped

600ml (1pt) milk

6 eggs

125g (4oz) caster sugar

Cream or crème fraîche to serve

For the coffee syrup

150g (5oz) granulated sugar

1 tbsp instant coffee, dissolved in 1 tbsp hot water

1 Put the chocolate in a bowl over a pan of simmering water with 2 tablespoons of the milk and heat until melted, stirring occasionally. Allow to cool slightly. Meanwhile beat the eggs and sugar together until they are fluffy. Bring the remaining milk to the boil, then remove it from the heat and add to the melted chocolate. Stir to combine, then pour the chocolate milk into the egg mixture, whisking continuously.

2 Preheat the oven to 160°C/325°F/gas 3. Put 8 buttered ramekins into a roasting tin. Strain the custard mixture into the ramekins, filling each one to the top. Pour hot water into the roasting tin so that it comes halfway up the sides of the ramekins, taking care not to splash water into the custards. Bake for about 30 minutes until firm but still a little wobbly in the centre. Remove from the tray and cool completely.

3 To make the coffee syrup, dissolve the sugar in 300ml (½ pint) water, bring to the boil and continue boiling until it is reduced by half. Stir in the liquid coffee and leave to cool. Run a knife round the inside of each ramekin and turn onto serving plates. Drizzle coffee syrup around them and serve with cream or crème fraîche.

Apple & lime Eve's pudding

Sticky sponge

Serves 6 **Preparation** 30 minutes + cooling **Cooking** 35 minutes

Ingredients

6 crisp dessert apples
125g (4oz) butter, melted
25g (1oz) caster sugar
Pinch of ground cinnamon
2 eggs
50g (2oz) soft light brown sugar
2 tbsp golden syrup
6 tbsp milk
225g (8oz) self-raising flour
Juice and finely grated zest of 2 limes

For the glaze

75g (3oz) sifted icing sugar
2 limes, juice only

1 Preheat the oven to 180°C/350°F/gas 4. Peel, quarter and core the apples then slice each quarter vertically so you have 8 pieces per apple. In 2 tablespoons of the butter, fry the apples with the sugar and cinnamon for 2–3 minutes. Remove from the heat.

2 Allow the caramelised apple pieces to cool a little then arrange them in a buttered 1.2–1.7 litre (2–3 pint) ovenproof baking dish in an even layer.

3 In a bowl, whisk the eggs with the soft light brown sugar and golden syrup until light and foamy. Stir in the remaining melted butter and the milk. Sift in the flour and mix it in with the lime juice and zest.

4 Pour the batter over the apples and bake for 25–30 minutes until the sponge is risen and golden. Sift the icing sugar into a small bowl and mix with the lime juice to form a runny paste. Spoon the icing over the warm pudding and serve.

Baker's tip
Warmed apricot jam and a dusting of icing sugar make a delicious alternative glaze.

Steamed chocolate pudding

Comfort dessert

Serves 4 **Preparation** 30 minutes **Cooking** 1 hour 35 minutes

Ingredients

175g (6oz) plain chocolate
1 tbsp sugar
5 tbsp milk
125g (4oz) butter
125g (4oz) light brown sugar
2 eggs, beaten
75g (3oz) self-raising flour
25g (1oz) cocoa powder
50g (2oz) chocolate chips

1 Butter a 1.7 litre (3 pint) pudding basin. Melt the chocolate and sugar in a bowl over a pan of simmering, but not boiling, water. Remove from the heat and stir in the milk. Pour into the base of the pudding basin.

2 Beat the butter and light brown sugar until combined. Add the eggs gradually, beating constantly. Sift the flour and cocoa powder together and gently stir into the mixture with the chocolate chips.

3 Spoon into the pudding basin and smooth the top. Cover with a sheet of greaseproof paper pleated along the centre to allow for expansion as the pudding cooks, then with a layer of pleated foil. Tie securely with string and place in a large pan.

4 Pour in boiling water to come halfway up the basin. Steam for 1 hour 30 minutes, until the pudding springs back when pressed lightly. Cool in the basin for a few minutes then turn out onto a warm serving plate.

Rhubarb & orange crumble

A true classic

Serves 6 **Preparation** 20 minutes **Cooking** 55 minutes

Ingredients

700g (1½lb) rhubarb, cut into 2.5cm (1in) pieces

1 piece stem ginger in syrup, drained and chopped

125g (4oz) caster sugar

3 oranges

For the topping

250g (9oz) plain flour

125g (4oz) butter, cubed

175g (6oz) caster sugar

1 Preheat the oven to 180°C/350°F/gas 4. Put the rhubarb and the chopped ginger into a 1.5 litre (2½ pint) ovenproof pie dish. Sprinkle over the caster sugar and 3 tablespoons water, cover with foil and cook in the oven for 15 minutes.

2 Meanwhile, grate the oranges and put the zest aside. Cut away the remaining skin and pith and slice into segments. Arrange the orange segments on top of the cooked rhubarb.

3 For the crumble topping, put the flour into a large bowl and stir in the orange zest. Add the butter and rub into the flour mixture with your fingertips. Stir in the sugar.

4 Pile crumble mix over the rhubarb and oranges, making sure the fruit is completely covered. Bake for 40 minutes until golden brown. Spoon crumble into dishes and serve with custard, cream or ice cream.

Baker's tip
Look for rhubarb with crisp, firm stalks which are not too large, with a rich pink colour.

Caramelised rice puddings

School dinners...

Makes 4 **Preparation** 15 minutes + cooling **Cooking** 1 hour 10 minutes

Ingredients

600ml (1pt) milk

50g (2oz) caster sugar

1 vanilla pod, split

50g (2oz) pudding rice

150ml (¼pt) double cream

4 tsp icing sugar

For the topping

125g (4oz) caster sugar

Juice of ½ lemon

1 tbsp cassis (blackcurrant liqueur)

225g (8oz) blueberries

Fresh mint sprigs to decorate

1 For the rice pudding, put the milk, sugar and vanilla pod into a saucepan. Heat slowly and bring to the boil. Stir in rice and bring back to the boil. Cover and simmer gently for about 1 hour, stirring regularly, to a thick consistency. Remove from heat, leave to cool. Chill.

2 Preheat the grill to high. Whip the cream until it forms soft peaks and lightly fold into chilled rice mixture. Spoon the rice into 6cm (2½in) round pastry cutters on a greased baking tray. Dust each pudding with 1 teaspoon icing sugar. Put the tray of puddings under the grill until the sugar caramelises and turns golden brown. Set aside and allow the caramel top to cool.

3 For the blueberry topping, heat 6 tablespoons water with the caster sugar in a saucepan until dissolved. Boil for 3-5 minutes. Add lemon juice and cassis. Reheat and bring slowly back to the boil. Add blueberries and simmer for 2 minutes. Set aside to cool.

4 Slide a palette knife under each pudding and transfer to a dessert plate. Spoon blueberry topping over the puddings. Decorate with sprigs of mint.

Apple strudel

Fruity favourite

Serves 6 **Preparation** 30 minutes **Cooking** 35 minutes

Ingredients

700g (1½lb) cooking apples, peeled, sliced and tossed in lemon juice
½ tsp ground cinnamon
½ tsp grated nutmeg
75g (3oz) raisins
125g (4oz) caster sugar
50g (2oz) pecans, chopped
1 lemon, juice and grated zest
4 sheets of frozen or chilled filo pastry, thoroughly defrosted
125g (4oz) unsalted butter, melted
50g (2oz) ground almonds
Flour, for sprinkling on the tea towel
Icing sugar for sprinkling

1 Preheat the oven to 220°C/425°F/gas 7. Line a baking sheet with baking parchment. Mix together the apples, spices, raisins, sugar, pecans, and the lemon zest and juice. Spread your first layer of filo pastry on a floured tea towel, brush with butter. Lay another sheet on top and brush with butter, repeat with the other sheets.

2 Sprinkle the ground almonds evenly over the top of the final sheet of buttered filo. Spread the fruit and nut filling along one long edge of the pastry, then fold the short ends in over the filling and the edge where you will begin rolling.

3 Start rolling up the pastry by turning in the border along the long edge nearest you. Keep rolling, lifting up the tea towel to help form the roll.

4 Before completing the roll, lift the far edge of the tea towel over the lined baking sheet and finish rolling the strudel carefully onto the tray, ending with it seam side down. Brush with butter. Bake for 30–35 minutes until crisp and golden. Sprinkle with icing sugar to serve.

Baker's tip

This recipe uses raisins, but for a slightly different flavour, try currants or sultanas.

!
CONTAINS
NUTS

Seville orange sponge

Gloriously gooey

Serves 4 **Preparation** 15 minutes + cooling **Cooking** 45 minutes

Ingredients

Juice of 2 oranges
50g (2oz) butter
125g (4oz) caster sugar
Grated zest of 1 orange
2 eggs, separated
75g (3oz) self-raising flour
3 tbsp Seville orange marmalade
4 tbsp milk

For the glaze

2 tbsp fine-cut or shredless Seville marmalade, to glaze

1 Preheat the oven to 190°C/375°F/gas 5. Butter a 900ml (1½ pint) pudding dish. Boil the orange juice to reduce by two-thirds then leave to cool.

2 Cream together the butter and caster sugar with the orange zest. Stir in the egg yolks, then the self-raising flour. Add the marmalade, milk and the reduced orange juice. Stir to combine.

3 Whisk the egg whites until they form soft peaks then gently fold into the pudding mix. Spoon into the dish and place the dish in a roasting tin. Pour hot water into the tin, approximately 1cm (½in) deep. Bake in the preheated oven for 40–45 minutes until golden brown.

4 To give an attractive glaze, mix the marmalade with 3–4 teaspoons water and warm together. Brush the glaze over the sponge and serve.

Queen of puddings

Serves 6 **Preparation** 40 minutes + cooling **Cooking** 1 hour 20 minutes

Ingredients

- 125g (4oz) unsalted butter, softened
- 125g (4oz) caster sugar
- 2 eggs
- 125g (4oz) self-raising flour
- 1 tsp baking powder
- 4 tbsp raspberry jam

For the custard

- 300ml (½pt) milk
- 300ml (½pt) double cream
- 1 vanilla pod
- 4 eggs
- 75g (3oz) caster sugar

For the meringue

- 4 egg whites
- 225g (8oz) caster sugar

1 Preheat the oven to 180°C/350°F/gas 4. Beat the sponge ingredients until blended. Spoon the mixture into a greased 18cm (7in) deep square cake tin, level the top and bake for 25 minutes. Turn out and cool. Slice the sponge horizontally into 3 layers and sandwich together with jam. Cut into small chunks and put a layer in the bases of 6 well buttered 7.5cm (3in) ramekins.

2 For the custard, pour the milk and cream into a pan. Split the vanilla pod and scrape in the seeds. Bring to the boil then take off the heat. Whisk the eggs and sugar lightly, then stir into the cooled milk. Strain through a sieve and pour over the sponge in the ramekins, just covering it.

3 Sit the ramekins in a roasting tin and add hot water half-way up the sides of the dishes. Cook for 30–40 minutes in a preheated oven at 170°C/325°F/gas 3, until the custard has set. Remove from the tin.

4 Increase the oven temperature to 220°C/425°F/gas 7. For the meringue, whisk the egg whites until they form soft peaks, then gradually whisk in the sugar until stiff and shiny. Pipe or spoon the meringue over the top of the puddings and return to the hot oven for 6 minutes until golden brown. Serve warm rather than hot.

Sticky toffee pudding

Winter warmer

Serves 8 **Preparation** 25 minutes **Cooking** 1 hour 5 minutes

Ingredients

275g (10oz) dates, stoned and chopped
450ml (15fl oz) water
125g (4oz) unsalted butter, softened
350g (12oz) light brown sugar
4 eggs, beaten
350g (12oz) self-raising flour
2 tsp bicarbonate of soda
2 tsp vanilla extract

For the toffee sauce

600ml (1pt) double cream
125g (4oz) demerara sugar
4 tsp black treacle

Baker's tip
After 45 minutes baking, if it looks well browned, lay a sheet of foil on top to prevent scorching.

1 Preheat the oven to 180°C/350°F/gas 4. Put the dates in a saucepan, pour over the water and simmer for about 5 minutes or until the dates are soft and paste-like. In a mixing bowl, cream the butter and light brown sugar together until pale. Beat in the eggs, a little at a time, adding a spoonful of the flour if the mixture looks as though it will curdle.

2 Add the bicarbonate of soda to the date paste – it will fizz up quite dramatically – and immediately add to the creamed mixture with the flour and vanilla, beating until all the ingredients are evenly combined. Pour the mixture into a 24cm x 24cm x 5cm (9½in x 9½in x 2in) baking dish and bake for 1 hour or until just firm to the touch.

3 For the sauce, put the cream, demerara sugar and treacle in a pan over a low heat and stir together until blended. Bring to the boil, simmer for 1 minute and serve hot poured over the hot pudding.

Warm ginger cake

Sticky & delicious

Serves 6 **Preparation** 15 minutes + cooling **Cooking** 1 hour

Ingredients

300g (11oz) plain flour
2 tsp bicarbonate of soda
2 tsp ground ginger
1 tsp ground cinnamon
¼ tsp ground mace
4 tbsp black treacle
4 tbsp golden syrup
150g (5oz) butter
50g (2oz) soft dark brown sugar
1 egg, beaten
150ml (¼pt) milk
1 piece stem ginger in syrup, to decorate

For the sauce

3 egg yolks
50g (2oz) caster sugar
Juice and finely grated zest of 2 lemons
125ml (4fl oz) dry sherry

1 Preheat the oven to 180°C/350°F/gas 4. Set a 20.5cm (8in) square deep cake pan onto a baking sheet. Sift the flour with the bicarbonate of soda and the spices into a bowl.

2 In a small saucepan melt the black treacle, golden syrup and the butter over a low heat and then stir in the brown sugar. Pour this into the flour mixture and beat well. Stir in the egg and milk and pour the batter into the pan.

3 Bake the ginger cake for 1 hour or until a skewer inserted into the middle comes out clean. Cool in the pan for 15 minutes then turn out and serve warm.

4 To make the lemon sauce, put the egg yolks and caster sugar into a bowl and whisk until the mixture turns thick and pale. Sit the bowl over a pan of simmering water and continue to whisk, gradually adding the lemon juice and finely grated zest and the dry sherry. Continue whisking until the sauce is warm and thick.

5 Serve the cake cut into squares with thinly sliced stem ginger arranged on top and a drizzle of lemon sauce.

Rum & banana bread pudding

Delicious dessert

Serves 6 **Preparation** 20 minutes + soaking **Cooking** 1 hour 15 minutes

Ingredients

450g (1lb) white bread or brioche, crusts removed

600ml (1pt) milk

125g (4oz) butter, melted, plus extra for greasing

175g (6oz) muscovado sugar, plus extra for the topping

2 eggs, beaten

4 bananas, halved lengthways and sliced, then tossed in 2 tbsp lemon juice

4 tbsp rum

50g (2oz) sultanas

1 tsp vanilla extract

½ tsp cinnamon

For the rum sauce

50g (2oz) butter

8 tbsp double cream

125g (4oz) caster sugar

2 tbsp rum

1 Preheat the oven to 180°C/350°F/gas 4. Chop or tear up the bread into a bowl, pour the milk over it and leave to soak for 30 minutes.

2 Beat the bread mixture until smooth. Stir the butter into the bread mixture with the sugar and eggs. Add the bananas, rum, sultanas and vanilla extract and mix thoroughly. Spoon the mixture into a 900g (2lb) loaf tin, greased and lined with baking parchment. Sprinkle the cinnamon and some muscovado sugar over the top.

3 Bake in the oven until golden on top. Turn out, remove the baking parchment and cool on a wire rack. Cut into 2.5cm (1in) slices.

4 To make the rum sauce, melt the butter in a saucepan. Then stir in the cream and sugar. Bring to a rolling boil, stirring constantly and remove from the heat. Stir in the rum and serve immediately.

Black Forest arctic roll

Frozen dessert delight

Serves 6 **Preparation** 45 minutes + freezing **Cooking** 15 minutes

Ingredients

125g (4oz) stoned bottled or canned cherries

600ml (1pt) vanilla ice cream

For the sponge

3 eggs

75g (3oz) caster sugar

50g (2oz) plain flour

1 tbsp cornflour

2 tbsp cocoa

For the sauce

150ml (¼pt) water

100g (3½oz) caster sugar

7 tbsp black cherry jam

Dash of kirsch (optional)

125g (4oz) stoned bottled or canned cherries

1 For the filling, dry the cherries with kitchen paper. Take the ice cream out of the freezer to soften slightly, then transfer to a bowl. Gently stir in the dry cherries until evenly distributed. Roll under plastic wrap into a 15cm (6in) long cylinder. Wrap in plastic wrap. Freeze overnight.

2 Preheat the oven to 180°C/350°/gas 4 and line a 33cm x 22cm (13in x 8½in) tin with baking parchment. In a large bowl, whisk the eggs and sugar until they are thick and pale and have tripled in volume. Sift together the flour, cornflour and cocoa, then gently fold into the egg mixture and pour into the tin. Bake for 12–15 minutes until springy to the touch. Cover the sponge with a damp cloth and leave to cool.

3 For the sauce, boil water and sugar until slightly syrupy. Add 3 tablespoons jam and kirsch (if using). Strain and mix with the cherries.

4 Uncover the sponge and turn out onto a sheet of baking parchment. Peel off the lining paper and trim the edges. Brush the remaining jam evenly over the surface. Lay the ice cream along the short end of the sponge and roll up until enclosed, trimming off any excess. Cover in plastic wrap and freeze for 30 minutes. Serve cut into slices with the cherry sauce.

Lemon & blackberry puddings

Fruity sponges

Serves 4 **Preparation** 15 minutes **Cooking** 35 minutes

Ingredients

250g (9oz) ripe blackberries

100g (3½oz) caster sugar, plus 1 tbsp

4 tbsp butter, softened

1 vanilla pod

Grated zest and juice of 1 large lemon

2 large eggs, separated

2 tbsp plain flour

250ml (9fl oz) milk

4 tbsp single cream, plus extra to serve

½ tsp cream of tartar

1 Put the blackberries and the one tablespoon of caster sugar in a bowl, toss gently, then spoon into 4 small, ovenproof dishes. Put the butter and the remaining sugar in a mixing bowl and beat until creamy. Split the vanilla pod, scrape the seeds into the mixture and beat into the mix.

2 Beat in the lemon zest, followed by the egg yolks. Sift in the flour, stir in, then gradually beat in the milk, cream and lemon juice. Put the egg whites and cream of tartar in a separate, grease-free bowl and whisk until stiff but not dry. Beat two tablespoons of the egg whites into the pudding mixture, then fold in the remainder with a spatula.

3 Spoon the mixture into the prepared dishes and bake in a preheated oven at 180°C/350°F/gas 4 for 30–35 minutes. Serve hot or warm.

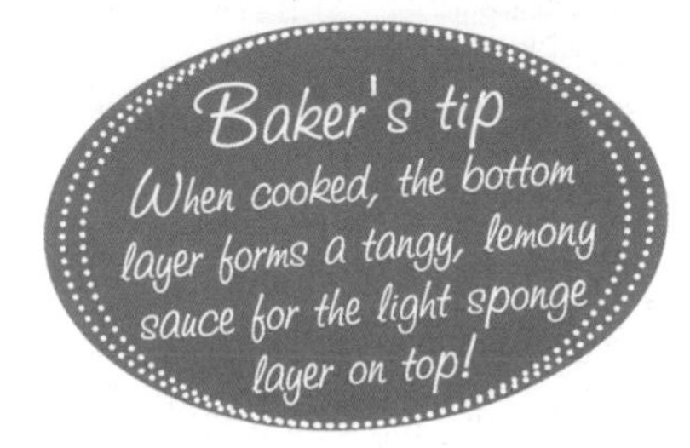

Steamed spotted dick

Fruity favourite

Serves 8 **Preparation** 20 minutes **Cooking** 1 hour

Ingredients

300g (11oz) plain flour
2 tsp baking powder
150g (5oz) caster sugar
125g (4oz) currants
Finely grated zest of 1–2 lemons
150g (5oz) shredded beef or vegetable suet
200ml (7fl oz) milk

1 Sift the flour and baking powder into a mixing bowl. Stir in 75g (3oz) of the sugar, with the currants, the lemon zest and the suet. Gradually stir in the milk to give a soft, moist dough. Using floured hands, work the dough into a ball, leaving the sides of the bowl clean.

2 Butter a sheet of greaseproof paper and sprinkle with 2 tablespoons sugar and place the dough on it. Using floured hands, shape into a 15–20.5cm (6–8in) long roll. Bring the long sides of the paper together, then fold 2 or 3 times to enclose the mixture. Leave some room for rising. Tie the ends with string.

3 Lower the parcel into a steamer set over a large pan of boiling water. Cover and steam for 1 hour. Check the water level regularly and top up with more boiling water from a kettle as necessary.

4 Remove the parcel from the steamer and unwrap the paper. Cut into 2.5cm (1in) thick slices. Serve at once with vanilla custard, drizzled with golden syrup or honey.

Baker's tip
Suet is the key to achieving the soft, closely packed texture. Grated shop-bought suet is ideal.